SIMON & GARFUNKEL: PIANO SOLO

Published by
Hal Leonard

Exclusive Distributors:

Hal Leonard 7777 West Bluemound Road, Milwaukee,
WI 53213 Email: info@halleonard.com

Hal Leonard Europe Limited 42 Wigmore Street
Maryleborne, London, W1U 2 RY
Email: info@halleonardeurope.com

Hal Leonard Australia Pty. Ltd.
4 Lentara Court Cheltenham,
Victoria, 9132 Australia
Email: info@halleonard.com.au

Order No. PS11726
ISBN: 978-1-78038-525-9
This book © Copyright 2012 Hal Leonard

Edited by Jenni Norey.
Music arranged by Derek Jones.
Music processed by Paul Ewers Music Design. Cover
design by Tim Field.

Printed in EU.

www.halleonard.com

SIMON & GARFUNKEL: PIANO SOLO

America

Words & Music by Paul Simon

♩. = 60

%

To Coda ⊕

cresc.

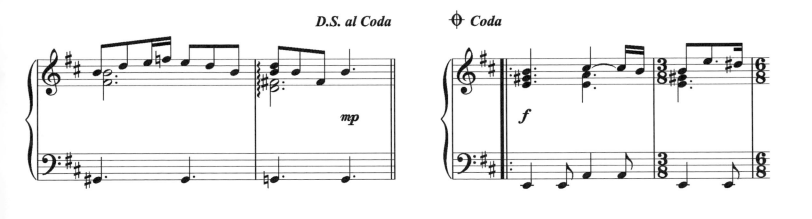

Play 3 times

The Boxer

Words & Music by Paul Simon

Play 4 times

13

Bridge Over Troubled Water

Words & Music by Paul Simon

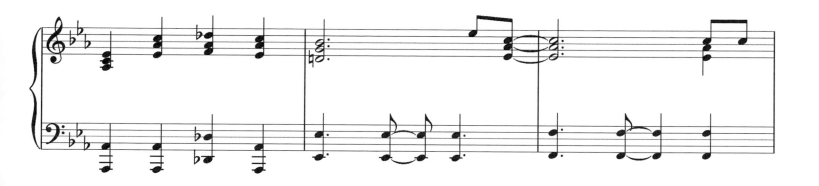

17

Cecilia

Words & Music by Paul Simon

The 59th Street Bridge Song
(Feelin' Groovy)

Words & Music by Paul Simon

Repeat ad infinitum   Optional ending

23

For Emily, Whenever I May Find Her

Words & Music by Paul Simon

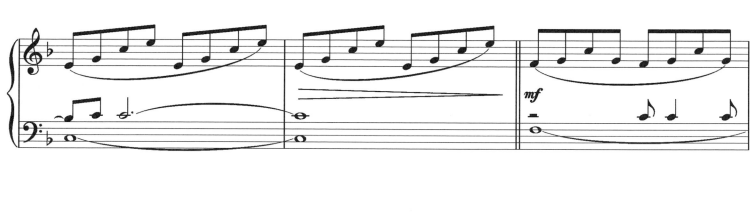

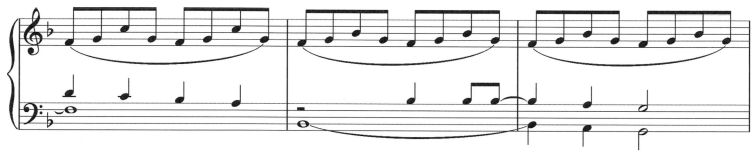

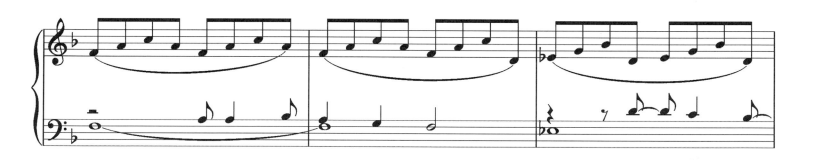

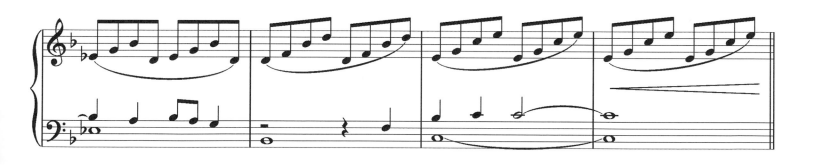

25

Homeward Bound

Words & Music by Paul Simon

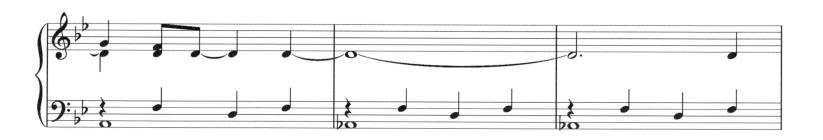

A Hazy Shade Of Winter

Words & Music by Paul Simon

I Am A Rock

Words & Music by Paul Simon

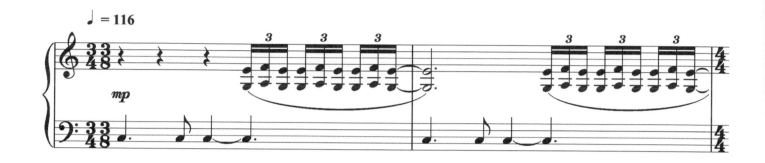

Mrs. Robinson

Words & Music by Paul Simon

D.S. al Coda

✛ *Coda*

Repeat ad lib. to fade

My Little Town

Words & Music by Paul Simon

Repeat ad lib. to fade

The Only Living Boy In New York

Words & Music by Paul Simon

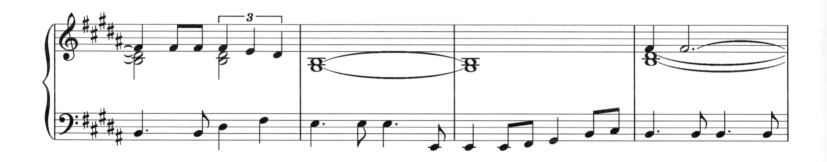

Scarborough Fair/Canticle

Traditional
Arrangement & Original Countermelody by Paul Simon & Art Garfunkel

The Sound Of Silence

Words & Music by Paul Simon

Con pedale

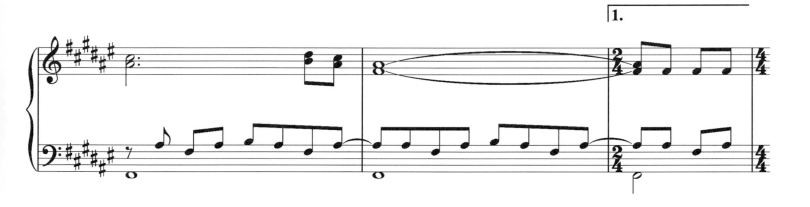

Wednesday Morning, 3 A.M.

Words & Music by Paul Simon

SIMON &
GARFUNKEL